Or[...]
Midnig[...] Wing

PHASE 3

/or/ur/
ow/

Level 4 – Blue

Helpful Hints for Reading at Home

The graphemes (written letters) and phonemes (units of sound) used throughout this series are aligned with Letters and Sounds. This offers a consistent approach to learning whether reading at home or in the classroom.

HERE IS A LIST OF NEW GRAPHEMES FOR THIS PHASE OF LEARNING. AN EXAMPLE OF THE PRONUNCIATION CAN BE FOUND IN BRACKETS.

Phase 3			
j (jug)	v (van)	w (wet)	x (fox)
y (yellow)	z (zoo)	zz (buzz)	qu (quick)
ch (chip)	sh (shop)	th (thin/then)	ng (ring)
ai (rain)	ee (feet)	igh (night)	oa (boat)
oo (boot/look)	ar (farm)	or (for)	ur (hurt)
ow (cow)	oi (coin)	ear (dear)	air (fair)
ure (sure)	er (corner)		

HERE ARE SOME WORDS WHICH YOUR CHILD MAY FIND TRICKY.

Phase 3 Tricky Words			
he	you	she	they
we	all	me	are
be	my	was	her

GPC focus: /or/ur/ow/

TOP TIPS FOR HELPING YOUR CHILD TO READ:

- Allow children time to break down unfamiliar words into units of sound and then encourage children to string these sounds together to create the word.

- Encourage your child to point out any focus phonics when they are used.

- Read through the book more than once to grow confidence.

- Ask simple questions about the text to assess understanding.

- Encourage children to use illustrations as prompts.

PHASE 3
/or/ur/ow/

This book focuses on the phonemes /or/, /ur/ and /ow/ and is a blue level 4 book band.

Orla and Midnight Wing

Written by
Kelby Twyman

Illustrated by
Sandra Stalker

Orla was looking at her book, Midnight Wing.

"You are a pain, Orla! Get up!"
Orla was in shock.

Carl was bad. "Orla, you are such a dork!"
Orla ran off up the path.

Orla was sad and ran into the wood.

Orla ran into a yurt. "I hurt my arm!"

Burt did a big burp and a big yell!
"That is my yurt!"

Burt was mad. "You cannot be in my yurt. Go!"

Orla got up. She was sad and hurt.

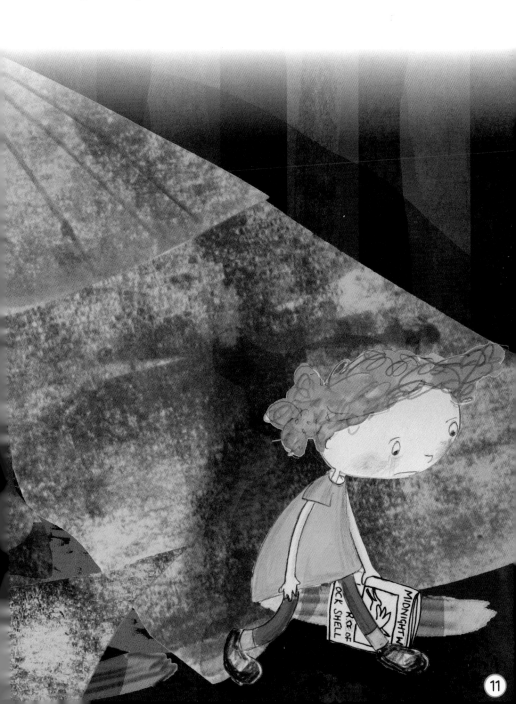

Burt was not mad. He was now sad for Orla.

"I wish I was Midnight Wing! I look up to him."

"Is Midnight Wing a turnip? Or is it a fish?"

Orla got her book. "No, look. This is Midnight Wing!"

"I will turn Orla into Midnight Wing.
Then she will not be sad."

Burt did a hop and got a horn. Orla was in shock.

"Orla, this horn will let you be Midnight Wing."

"No, Burt! That is not the right horn!"

"Midnight Wing is quick. He can jet off into the night."

Burt ran to his yurt and put a jet pack on Orla.

"No, no! I will not jet off with that on me!"

Burt put the jet pack on his back. "I will jet off!"

A huff and a burp and then a big burn!
"My yurt, my yurt!"

"Look at the yurt burn!" Orla was sad for Burt.

Orla was sad. "I will not get to be Midnight Wing!"

"Orla, you will be Midnight Wing." Burt ran to his hut, deep in the wood.

"This is it. This is it!" A big light, a big pop, and then a big burp!

Burt ran to Orla. "Look Orla, you are Midnight Wing!"

Orla and Midnight Wing

1. Who made fun of Orla?

2. Who did Orla find in the wood?

3. What burned down the yurt?
    (a) Dragon
    (b) Jet pack
    (c) Fireworks

4. What did Burt bring to Orla at the end?

5. Who do you look up to? Who would you want to be like?

©2021 **BookLife Publishing Ltd.**
King's Lynn, Norfolk PE30 4LS

ISBN 978-1-83927-397-1

All rights reserved. Printed in Malaysia.
A catalogue record for this book is available
from the British Library.

Orla and Midnight Wing
Written by Kelby Twyman
Illustrated by Sandra Stalker

An Introduction to BookLife Readers...

Our Readers have been specifically created in line with the London Institute of Education's approach to book banding and are phonetically decodable and ordered to support each phase of Letters and Sounds.

Each book has been created to provide the best possible reading and learning experience. Our aim is to share our love of books with children, providing both emerging readers and prolific page-turners with beautiful books that are guaranteed to provoke interest and learning, regardless of ability.

BOOK BAND GRADED using the Institute of Education's approach to levelling.

PHONETICALLY DECODABLE supporting each phase of Letters and Sounds.

EXERCISES AND QUESTIONS to offer reinforcement and to ascertain comprehension.

BEAUTIFULLY ILLUSTRATED to inspire and provoke engagement, providing a variety of styles for the reader to enjoy whilst reading through the series.

AUTHOR INSIGHT:
KELBY TWYMAN

Inspired by books he read growing up, Kelby Twyman has always loved using the power of his imagination to create stories full of adventure. He grew up in a small village surrounded by animals and a dog called Jessie, who he often went on adventures with. Kelby obtained a business degree from a Cambridge-based university. This led him into a career in marketing for children's books. Kelby enjoys stories that have a moral compass and teach right from wrong. He likes to reflect this in his own writing, whether it be in his stories, poems or blogs. Kelby is excited to start his very own adventure writing books for BookLife Publishing.

PHASE 3
/or/ur/
ow/

This book focuses on the phonemes /or/, /ur/ and /ow/ and is a blue level 4 book band.

31